Made in the USA
Columbia, SC
23 October 2022

69881105R00083